KAVYADOSE

INSPIRATIONAL QUOTES

DEVENDRA KHOT

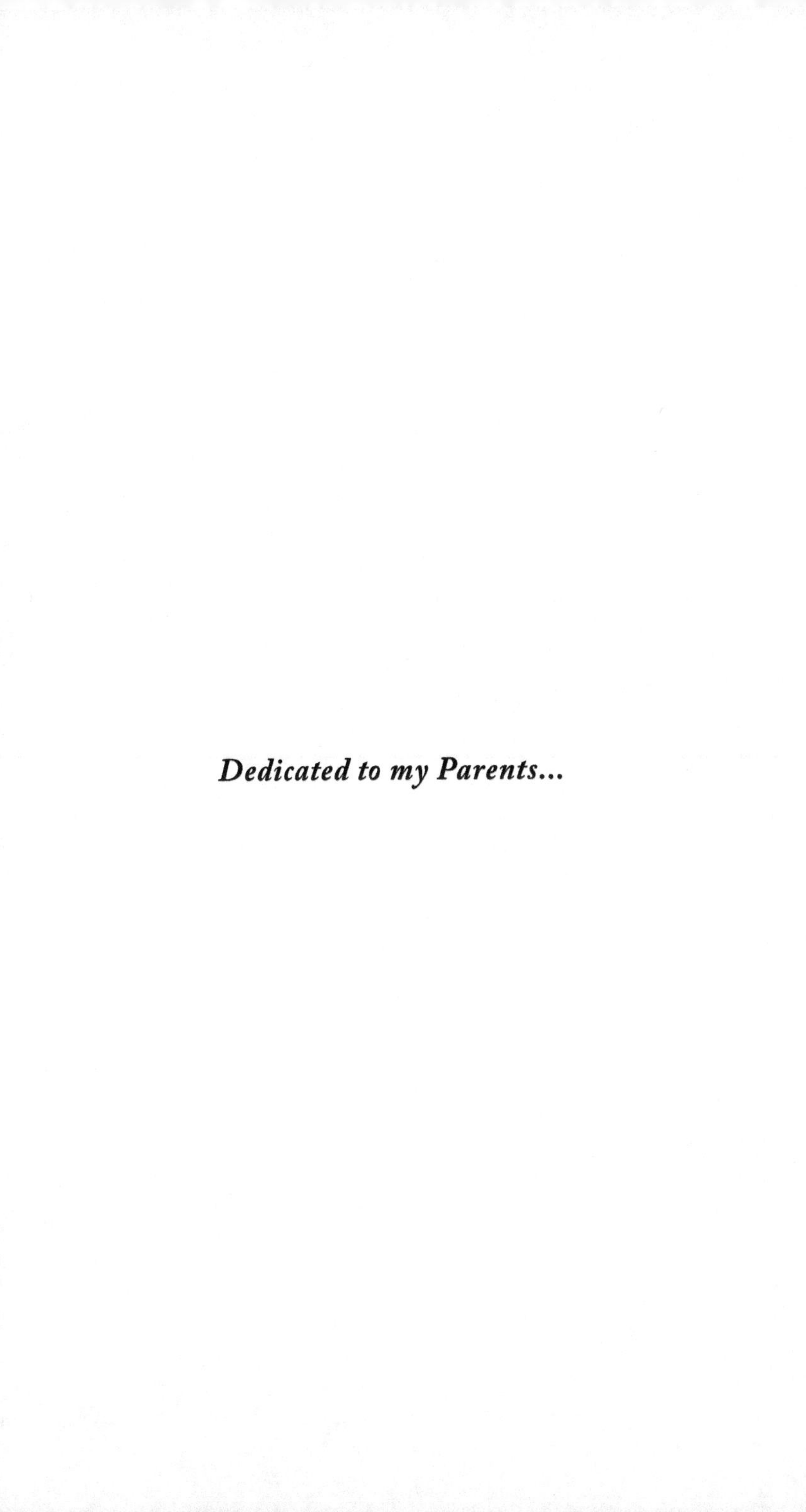

Dedicated to my Parents...

Contents

Acknowledgements   *vii*

Part 1

Acknowledgements

I am extremely grateful to ***"YourQuote App"*** for their wonderful images and other app features that inspired me for writing in accordance to the image.

One day, there'll be
nothing to worry
so why are you bothered
today, unnecessary !!!

— Devendra Khot

Life can be exactly how we want it to be if we be flexible for changes...and not be stiff !

- Devendra Khot

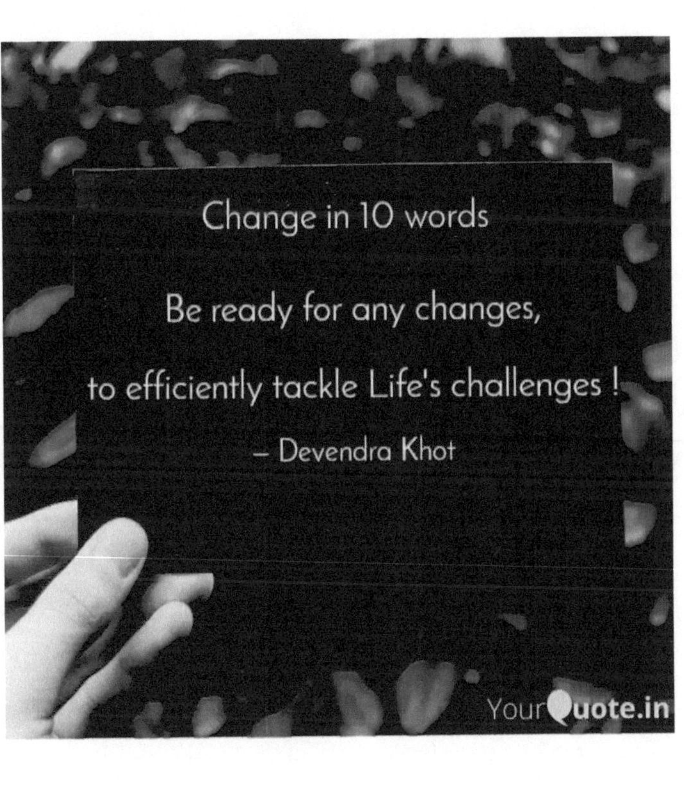

Change in 10 words
Be ready for any changes,
to efficiently tackle Life's challenges !
— Devendra Khot
YourQuote.in

My daydreams often involve

going beyond a stop,

where others thinking

and efforts get a full Stop !!!

— Devendra Khot

(A Challenge by Aesthetic Thoughts)

YourQuote.in

Ice-cream makes me believe
that only way to relieve ..
is keeping yourself chilled
when HOT anger is filled !!!

– Devendra Khot

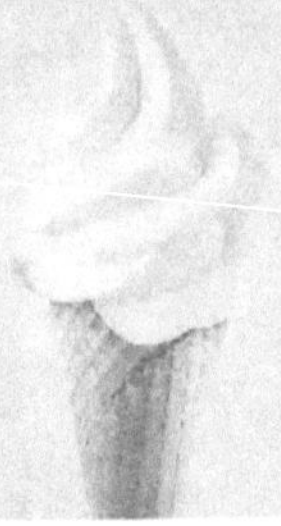

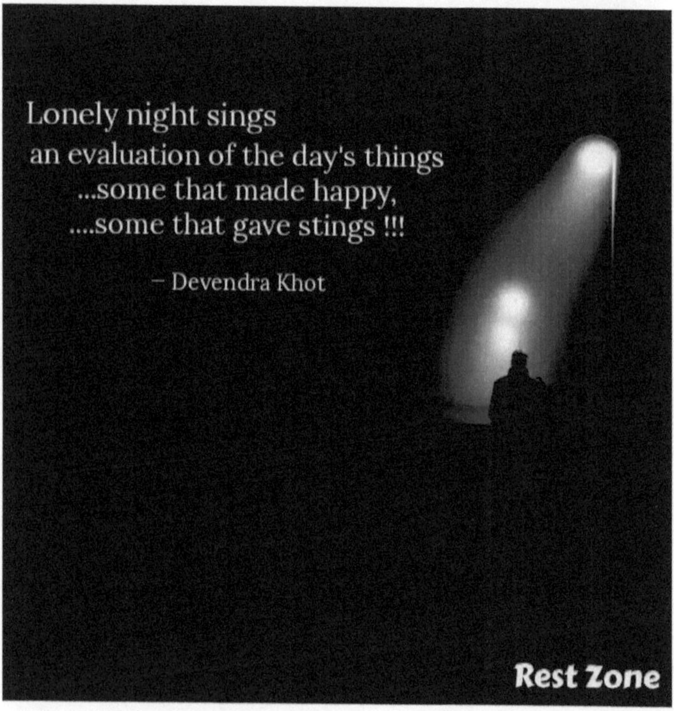

Lonely night sings
an evaluation of the day's things
...some that made happy,
....some that gave stings !!!

– Devendra Khot

Rest Zone

Time is like that friend who
will be with you forever.
Behave with him properly,
and loose the friendship never !!!

— Devendra Khot

Life is like a sea....
deep to understand from the shore...
just lit the hopes , then you will see,
even in the dusk... more and more.....

Devendra Khot

(A Challenge by Aesthetic Thoughts)

There's more to life than

just keeping on complaining !

Think and live positively,

and see your Life gaining !!!

– Devendra Khot

The ruled pages of life

guide us to live better,

and never to shatter,

whatever be the matter !!!

— *Devendra Khot*

You need not fly

if time has made you cry...

but afterwards you should again give a try,

and take a leap of success in the sky !!!

— Devendra Khot

Rest Zone

It's a funny thing about life
that we think about past and future,
and in the process forget,
our 'present time' to nurture !!

– Devendra Khot

YourQuote.in

I wait for tomorrow as if
everything will be right,
but in the process forgetting,
that 'Today' was the real fight !!!
— Devendra Khot
YourQuote.in

Time is like that friend who
will be with you forever.
Behave with him properly,
and loose the friendship never !!!

– Devendra Khot

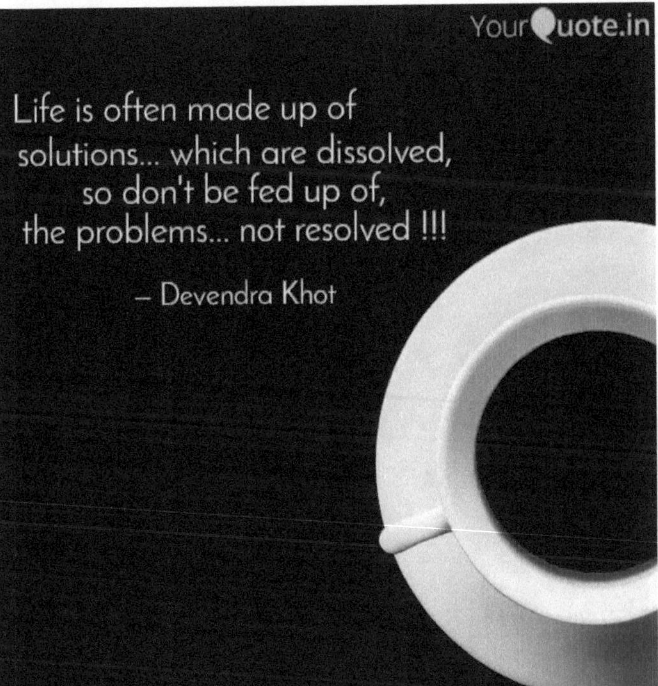
YourQuote.in

Life is often made up of
solutions... which are dissolved,
so don't be fed up of,
the problems... not resolved !!!

- Devendra Khot

Nights make me believe

that never fade away,

and loose the spark,

like the stars in the dark !!!

— Devendra Khot

When life dries

......don't give up your tries,

success will shower from the skies,

and see a greener life with your eyes !!!

— Devendra Khot

(A Challenge by Aesthetic Thoughts)

I found hope
....when all was sinking
failure got a nope
....with just 'Positive thinking' !!!

=Devendra Khot

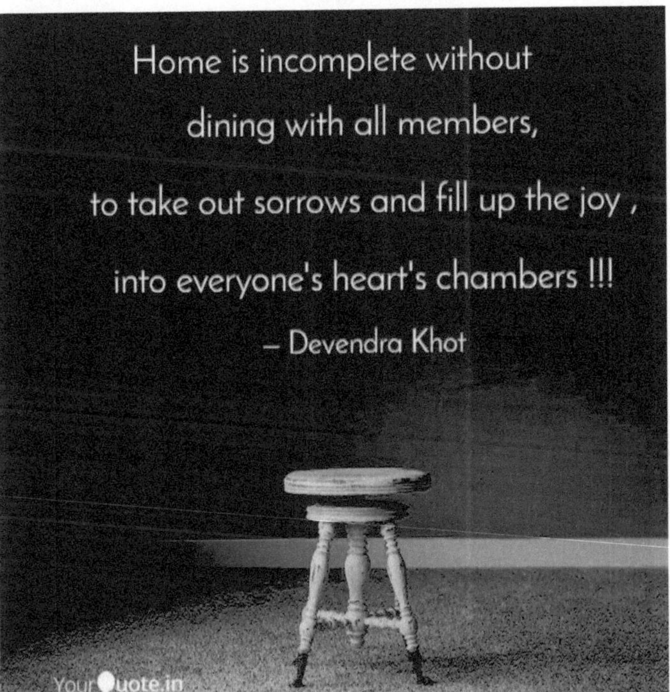

Home is incomplete without
dining with all members,
to take out sorrows and fill up the joy ,
into everyone's heart's chambers !!!
– Devendra Khot
YourQuote.in

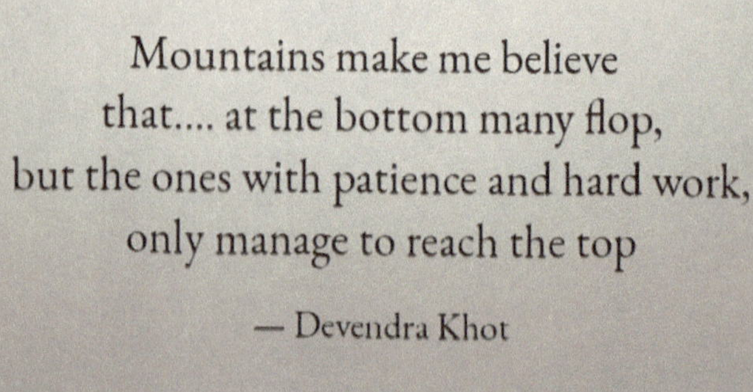

Mountains make me believe
that.... at the bottom many flop,
but the ones with patience and hard work,
only manage to reach the top

— Devendra Khot

YourQuote.in

Being slow isn't about

doubting your capability

but

it's a test of situation handling ability

— Devendra Khot

*To move on in life
is a real skill ...
and it all depends
on your positive will !!!*

— Devendra Khot

There's always something good
you have to see with 'that' vision..
otherwise you'll keep complaining
with one or other reason !!!

— Devendra Khot

Life appears to be bright when

you keep aside your fright,

and use all your might....

to bring success in your sight !!!

— Devendra Khot

Imperfections are

...a guide to us ,

which like 'teachers',

fine tune us !!!

— Devendra Khot

There is only one rule of living, and that is
the art of giving..

– Devendra Khot

YourQuote.in

The beauty of time is
that ...its with you forever,
but neglecting it ....
.......comes back never !!!
– Devendra Khot
YourQuote.in

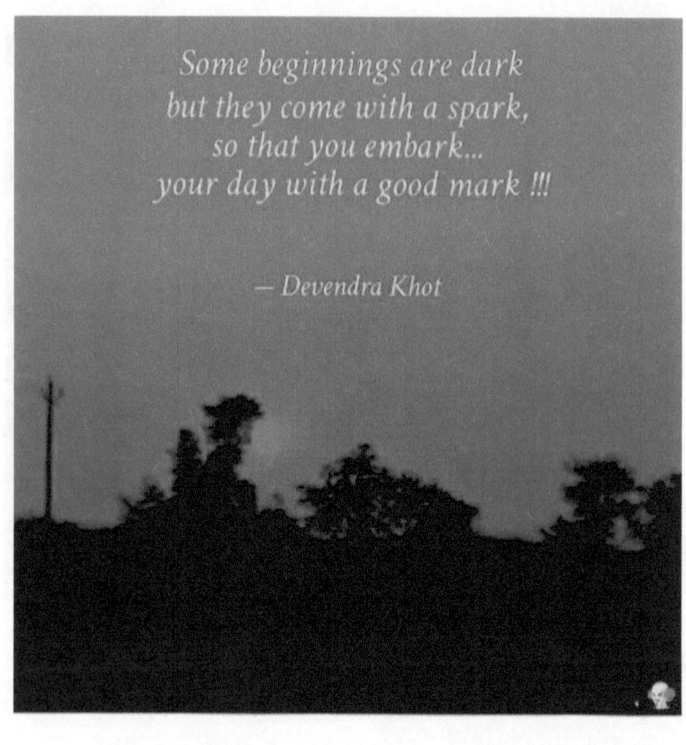

Some beginnings are dark
but they come with a spark,
so that you embark...
your day with a good mark !!!

— Devendra Khot

A new hope
is always there..
just keep aside
your worry and fear !!!

— Devendra Khot

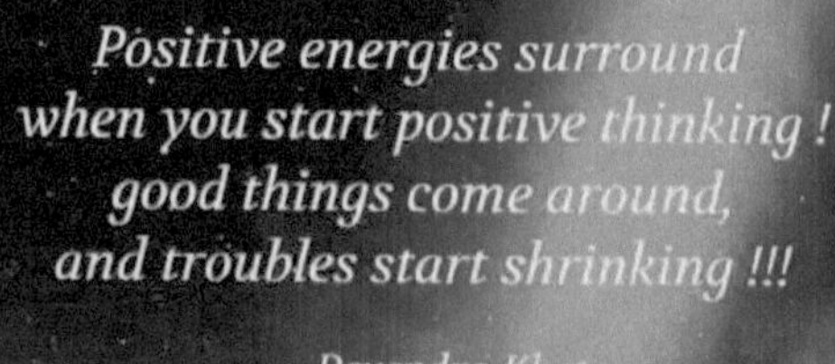

Positive energies surround
when you start positive thinking !
good things come around,
and troubles start shrinking !!!

— Devendra Khot

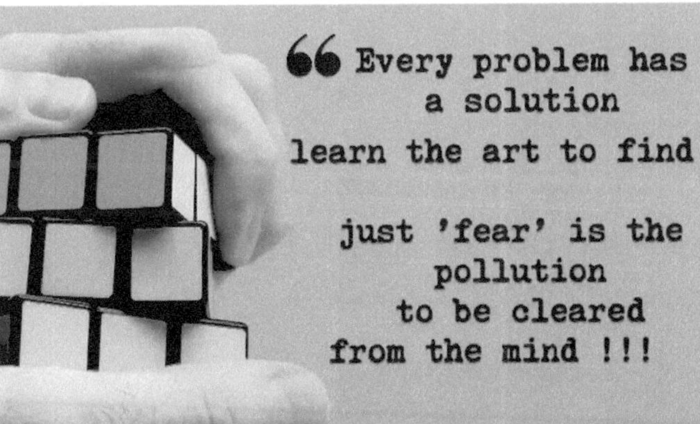

Every problem has
a solution
learn the art to find

just 'fear' is the
pollution
to be cleared
from the mind ! ! !

- Devendra Khot

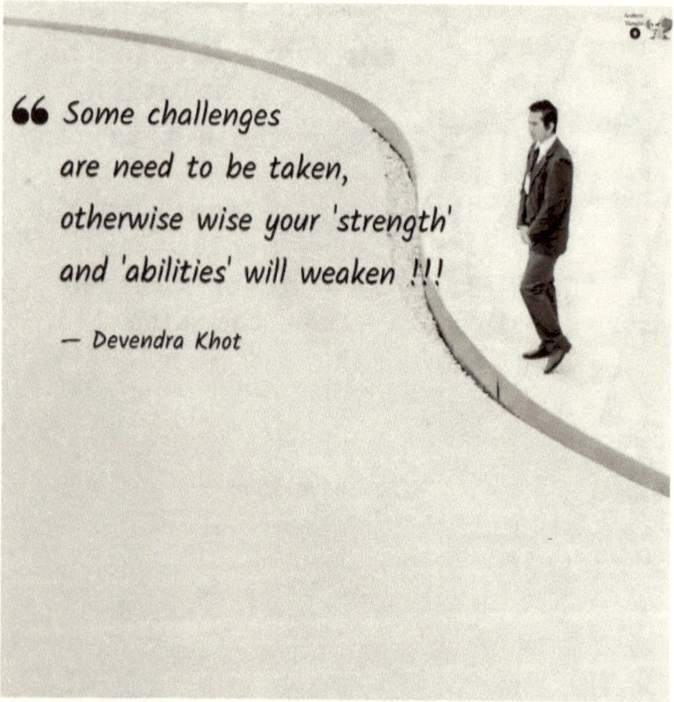

❝ Some challenges are need to be taken, otherwise wise your 'strength' and 'abilities' will weaken !!!

— Devendra Khot

Life was never easy
nor was feather lite,
just keep yourself busy
and continue enjoying your fight !!!

— Devendra Khot

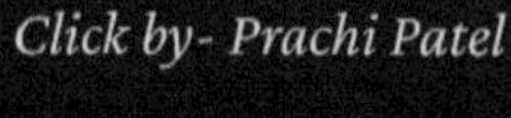

Click by- Prachi Patel

Celebrate the moment
no past or future comment
to keep away any lament
and feel real enjoyment !!!

— Devendra Khot

Rest Zone

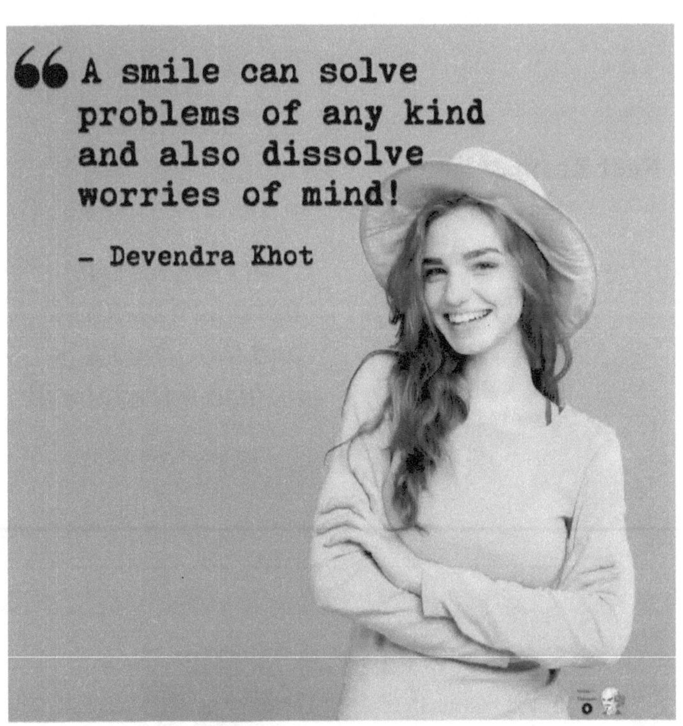
A smile can solve
problems of any kind
and also dissolve
worries of mind!

- Devendra Khot

Rest Zone

*Art enables us
unlimited pleasure
and the artwork is
invaluable treasure !!!*

— Devendra Khot

Every morning is a new page
just come out from yesterday's cage!
Start your day with a positive image,
so that your planned work don't get a damage!

— Devendra Khot

Rest Zone

Soar like never before
to reach the goal you set !
Work like never before,
till your goal of life is ....met !!!

— Devendra Khot

Rest Zone

Music is a tool
that satisfies you in full
keeps you .....cool
and gives happiness a pull !!!

— Devendra Khot

Failure in 8 Words

You may fall.......
if your efforts are small !!!

— Devendra Khot

No race is tough...
just keep going
real courage lies in the,
process of undergoing !!!

— Devendra Khot

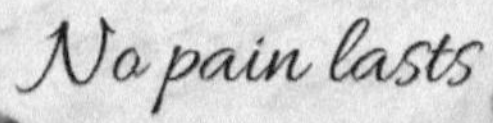

..... No pain will last,
just make your energy vast
so that you can outlast ,
.......the pain ...very fast !!!

– Devendra Khot

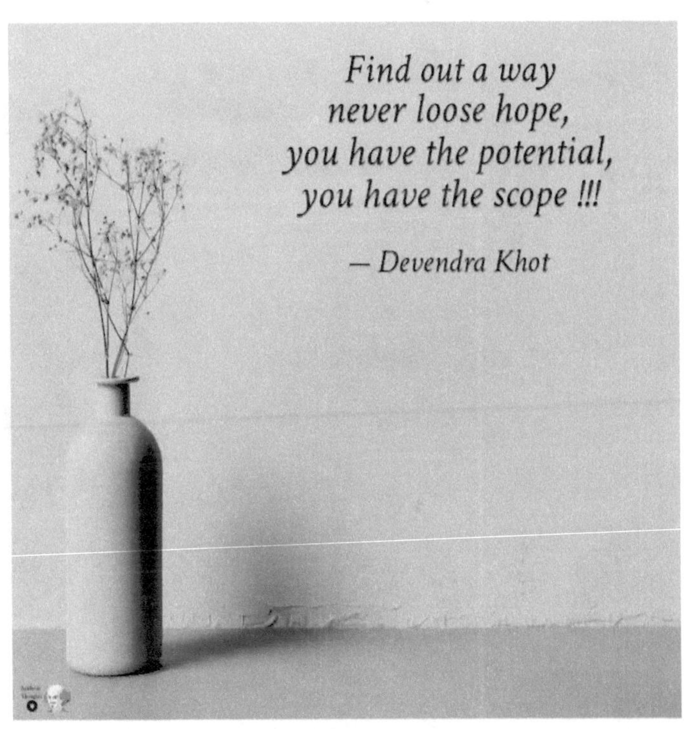

Find out a way
never loose hope,
you have the potential,
you have the scope !!!

— Devendra Khot

To design one's life
brush up the sorrow,
and the colours of joy,
will automatically follow !!!

— Devendra Khot

The life of a human
.....is like dust,
which doesn't settle,
and keeps moving just !!.

— Devendra Khot

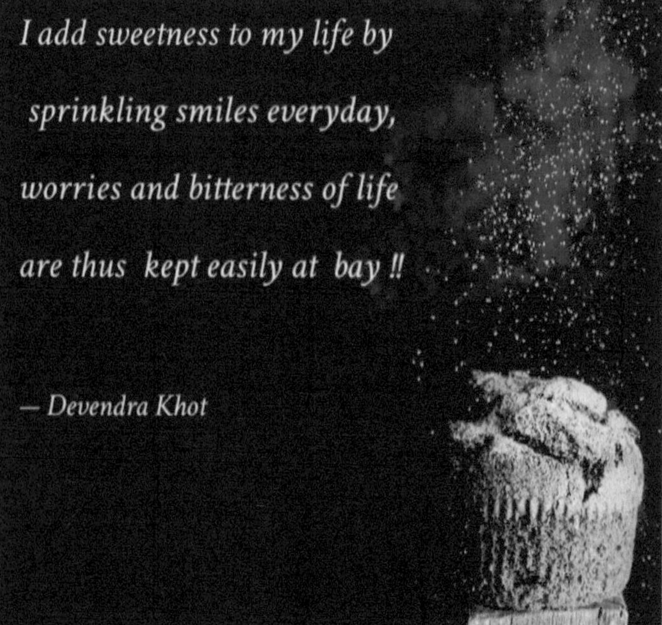

I add sweetness to my life by
sprinkling smiles everyday,
worries and bitterness of life
are thus kept easily at bay !!

— Devendra Khot

I define victory as
...achieving a dream
and a sense of satisfaction
flowing in my bloodstream !

- Devendra Khot

The music of nature
dwells everywhere !
...with an empty mind,
just be there !!!

— Devendra Khot

Positivity is a nourishment

negativity is a punishment !!!

— Devendra Khot

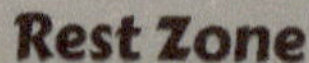

Rest Zone

Happiness can be found
.....all around
just change the vision,
if worries surround !!!

— Devendra Khot

Beauty can be found
all around....
in the nature's view,
in the nature's sound !

— Devendra Khot

More 'KavyaDose' parts on various topics like Life inspiration, social issues, health in English and Marathi....coming soon

-Devendra Khot

B.Pharm, MBA

Sangli,Maharashtra ,India

9372909099

madhumitradiabetes@gmail.com

www.ingramcontent.com/pod-product-compliance
Lightning Source LLC
Chambersburg PA
CBHW021140130726
47988CB00003B/1394